MALALA YOUSAFZAI

Caitie McAneney

New York

Published in 2017 by The Rosen Publishing Group, Inc.
29 East 21st Street, New York, NY 10010

First Edition

Editor: Katie Kawa
Book Design: Reann Nye

Photo Credits: Cover, pp. 1–32 (halftone pattern) Solomin Andrey/Shutterstock.com; cover, pp. 1, 7 Christopher Furlong/Getty Images News/Getty Images; p. 5 Andreas Rentz/ Getty Images Entertainment/Getty Images; p. 9 ADEK BERRY/AFP/Getty Images; pp. 11, 13, 15 Veronique de Viguerie/Getty Images News/Getty Images; p. 16 Adam Bettcher/ Getty Images Entertainment/Getty Images; p. 17 AFP/Getty Images; p. 19 Handout/Getty Images News/ Getty Images; p. 21 STAN HONDA/AFP/Getty Images; p. 23 JStone/Shutterstock.com; p. 24 AAMIR QURESHI/AFP/Getty Images; p. 25 ODD ANDERSEN/AFP/Getty Images; p. 27 Nigel Waldron/Getty Images Entertainment/Getty Images; p. 29 Chip Somodevilla/ Getty Images News/Getty Images; p. 30 CORNELIUS POPPE/AFP/Getty Images.

Library of Congress Cataloging-in-Publication Data

Cataloging-in-Publication Data

McAneney, Caitie.
Malala Yousafzai / by Caitie McAneney.
p. cm. — (Super women role models)
Includes index.
ISBN 978-1-5081-4833-3 (pbk.)
ISBN 978-1-5081-4775-6 (6-pack)
ISBN 978-1-5081-4808-1 (library binding)
1. Yousafzai, Malala, — 1997 — Juvenile literature. 2. Girls — Education — Pakistan — Juvenile literature. 3. Women human rights workers — Pakistan — Biography — Juvenile literature. I. McAneney, Caitie. II. Title.
LC2330.M384 2016
371.822095491—d23

Manufactured in the United States of America

CPSIA Compliance Information: Batch #BS16PK: For Further Information contact Rosen Publishing, New York, New York at 1-800-237-9932

CONTENTS

CHANGING THE WORLD FOR WOMEN

How can one teenage girl change the world? In a time when girls are silenced in her home country of Pakistan, Malala Yousafzai's voice rings out across the globe. She fights for women's rights, especially the right to an education. In 2014, she was awarded the Nobel Peace Prize, which made her the youngest person ever to receive that famous award.

Malala's speeches and writings are regarded as important works of **activism**. In 2012, standing up for the right for girls and women to be educated nearly cost Malala her life, but she soon became an international symbol of courage and hope for girls and women everywhere. Malala has inspired people through her bravery and her belief that girls and women can make a difference in the world.

IN HER WORDS

"Sometimes people like to ask me why should girls go to school, why is it important for them? But I think the more important question is why shouldn't they? Why shouldn't they have this right to go to school?"
Nobel Lecture delivered in Oslo, Norway, on December 10, 2014

Even the most important world leaders listen to Malala's ideas on girls' and women's rights.

FAST LEARNER

Malala was born July 12, 1997, in Mingora, which is a town in the Swat Valley of Pakistan. Usually, only the birth of sons is formally recognized in Pakistan. However, Malala's father, Ziauddin, put her name in the family records, showing that he believed she was just as important as a son. He and his wife named her Malala, after a **Pashtun** female hero.

Ziauddin had a firm belief that girls should have the same education as boys. Before Malala was born, he opened a school to educate girls and help them become leaders.

From a young age, Malala was a fast learner. When she was only two years old, she attended classes with students eight years older than she was. As she grew older, Malala earned the highest grades in her classes.

ZIAUDDIN YOUSAFZAI

Perhaps Malala's greatest supporter is her father, Ziauddin. When Ziauddin was young, he thought it was unfair that he was able to get an education, but his sisters couldn't. In 1994, Ziauddin opened the Khushal Girls High School and College. He inspired Malala's activism by taking her to anti-Taliban rallies and standing beside her as she gave speeches about education. In December 2012, Ziauddin was named the United Nations (UN) Special Adviser on Global Education. He works as a Pakistani **diplomat** in the United Kingdom, specializing in education.

Had Malala been born to any other family, she may not have had the opportunity to go to school. Her father believed in educating girls, which is an idea not everyone in Pakistan supports.

WHAT IS THE TALIBAN?

Pakistan is a democratic country that has positive ties with the United States. However, it's also home to a **militant** Islamic group called Tehrik-i-Taliban Pakistan, or the Pakistani Taliban. In 2007, the Pakistani Taliban formed from smaller militant groups. Their goal is to replace the democratic law in Pakistan with Sharia law, or Islamic law.

While they're an Islamic group, the Taliban's cruel and hateful practices don't reflect the beliefs of most people who practice Islam, which has over 1.5 billion followers worldwide. Members of the Taliban believe women shouldn't be able to go to school. They enforce what they see as the law with harsh punishments, often death. They attempted to kill Malala for speaking out about the right for all girls to be educated.

SHARIA LAW

The holy book of the Islamic religion, which is called the Qur'an, is one of the foundations of Sharia law. Sharia is the moral code and law of Islam, which covers diet, prayer, politics, and more. While most Muslims, or people who follow Islam, interpret the Qur'an as a peaceful text and Sharia as a personal code of living, some **extremists** punish those who don't follow their strict understanding of Sharia.

A burka is a piece of women's clothing that covers the entire body, including the face. While many **conservative** Muslim women choose to wear burkas for various reasons, the Taliban forced women in Pakistan to wear them.

LIFE UNDER TALIBAN RULE

The Taliban carried out bombings and other **terrorist** acts throughout Pakistan, including Malala's home of Swat Valley. They closed down schools for girls and women.

Many people in Pakistan were scared into silence. One word against the Taliban could cost them their life. However, Malala and her father knew it was important to speak out against this terrorist group and tell the world that girls and women deserve the right to go to school.

In September 2008, 11-year-old Malala traveled with her father to Peshawar, the capital city of their region of Pakistan. She stood up at a protest and gave a speech, which was entitled "How Dare the Taliban Take Away My Basic Right to Education?"

IN HER WORDS

"The extremists are afraid of books and pens. The power of education frightens them. They are afraid of women. The power of the voice of women frightens them."

Speech to the UN Youth Assembly, delivered in New York City on July 12, 2013

By making that first speech, Malala stood up for her right to have a voice in society. It was a very dangerous—but very important—thing to do.

A BRAVE BLOG

Malala's speech could do nothing to stop the Taliban's cruelty. In late 2008, they shut down all girls' schools in Pakistan. They bombed many of the girls' schools in Malala's hometown. However, Malala didn't give up.

The British **Broadcasting** Company (BBC) asked Malala's father to find someone to write a **blog** for them about life under the Taliban's control. Malala agreed to write blog posts under the name Gul Makai to keep her identity safe.

Nearly every day, Malala would write about how the Taliban's grip was tightening on her town. She wrote about schools closing, not being able to leave home, and her friends leaving. She wrote of being bored at home and of the fear many felt around her.

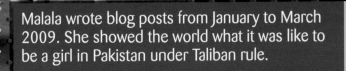

Malala wrote blog posts from January to March 2009. She showed the world what it was like to be a girl in Pakistan under Taliban rule.

FILMING FEARLESSLY

Malala soon moved beyond just writing blog posts. She also agreed to be on television, which was very risky because she couldn't do that while keeping her identity secret. She appeared on a news show in Pakistan called *Capital Talk* in February 2009. Malala soon became a very visible education activist who was known around the world.

In 2009, Malala also agreed to work on a short **documentary** called *Class Dismissed: The Death of Female Education*. Produced by *New York Times* reporter Adam Ellick, the documentary shows members of the Taliban harming people in Swat Valley and blowing up buildings. In the documentary, Malala sits by her father and says, "I want to get my education, and I want to become a doctor," before she begins to cry. The *New York Times* also released a second documentary featuring Malala, which is called *A Schoolgirl's Odyssey*.

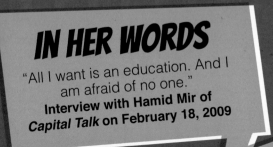

IN HER WORDS

"All I want is an education. And I am afraid of no one."
Interview with Hamid Mir of
Capital Talk **on February 18, 2009**

When many people wanted to hide out of fear of the Taliban, Malala was brave and shared her thoughts with the world. She wanted to do what she could to make Pakistan a better place for girls and women such as the ones shown here.

IDENTITY UNCOVERED

A *Schoolgirl's Odyssey* shows the beginnings of Malala's political efforts. In the documentary, she meets with Richard Holbrooke, the top U.S. official in Pakistan. At only 12 years old, she asked Holbrooke to help her fight for educational equality in Pakistan.

After the documentaries and television appearances aired, Malala's identity was discovered. When Malala returned to Swat Valley, she was in danger. Her father was also in danger of being harmed by members of the Taliban.

Malala attracted the attention of the Taliban, but she also attracted the attention of Pakistani and world leaders. Pakistan's first National Youth Peace Prize went to Malala in December 2011. Her country recognized the important things she was doing.

DESMOND TUTU

Desmond Tutu, who's a famous South African human rights activist, nominated Malala for the International Children's Peace Prize in 2011. She didn't win that year, but she did win the award in 2013.

Malala is shown here in 2013 with her International Children's Peace Prize. Malala is a role model for young people around the world.

SHOT BUT NOT SILENCED

Malala was able to return to school by February 2009, but she had to wear a burka. Women had to wear them everywhere they went out of fear of the Taliban.

On October 9, 2012, Malala and her classmates left school and boarded a truck that was being used as a school bus. Shortly after, a man with a gun boarded the bus. He asked for Malala. When he found her, he shot her in the head. He shot other girls on the bus, too.

The bullet passed through Malala's head, neck, and shoulder. Malala was rushed to a Pakistani hospital. Her brain began to swell, so surgeons had to put a metal plate in her head. Then, she was flown from Pakistan to Birmingham, England, for more medical treatment.

Malala is pictured here with her father and one of her younger brothers during her time in the hospital in England. Her family was by her side to help her through her recovery.

MIRACLE RECOVERY

When Malala woke up after being put into a coma, or deep sleep, she couldn't speak right away. However, she seemed to want to communicate with the nurses and doctors around her. The hospital staff brought her a board with letters on it, and she pointed to them to make words. Later, they brought her a notebook so she could ask and answer questions. This was good news—it meant her mental abilities weren't harmed.

However, the left side of Malala's face was paralyzed, or unable to move, so she had to go through a 10-hour operation to fix it. She continued to recover in England. Then, on July 12, 2013, Malala stood on stage at the UN headquarters in New York City for her first public appearance since she was shot.

IN HER WORDS

"They thought that the bullets would silence us. But they failed. And then, out of that silence came thousands of voices."
Speech to the UN Youth Assembly, delivered in New York City on July 12, 2013

Malala's UN speech on July 12, 2013, marked another life milestone, too. It was her 16th birthday.

IN THE SPOTLIGHT

The attack on Malala by the Taliban put her in the international spotlight. It was clear that this young woman was a role model for people young and old and a leader in the fight for global education. In fact, Malala was named one of *Time* magazine's most influential people in 2013.

That same year, Malala was awarded the United Nations Human Rights Prize. The UN awards this prize every five years to people and organizations that make a major difference in the fight for human rights. In 2014, the National Constitution Center in Philadelphia, Pennsylvania, gave Malala the Liberty Medal for her fight for freedom of education. She became the youngest person to ever receive this award.

IN HER WORDS

"The terrorists thought that they would change our aims and stop our ambitions but nothing changed in my life except this: Weakness, fear, and hopelessness died. Strength, power, and courage was born."
Speech to the UN Youth Assembly, delivered in New York City on July 12, 2013

Malala has become known throughout the world for having the courage to stand up for what she believes in—even when it puts her in danger.

WRITING HER STORY

Malala's great ability to express herself through speaking and writing made everyone—from students to world leaders—want to hear what she had to say. In 2013, Malala wrote a **memoir**, with help from Christina Lamb of the British newspaper the *Sunday Times*, to give people a deeper look into her life and her ideas.

Malala's memoir is entitled *I Am Malala: The Girl Who Stood Up for Education and Was Shot by the Taliban*. In the book, she describes her experience as a schoolgirl, as a target of the Taliban, and now, as an activist. Malala also addresses the importance of education for the future of women in countries such as Pakistan. Unfortunately, the book was banned in private schools in her home country.

IN HER WORDS

"I told myself, Malala, you have already faced death. This is your second life. Don't be afraid — if you are afraid, you can't move forward."
I Am Malala

Millions of people have read *I Am Malala*. This book has spread Malala's message of educational equality to readers all over the world.

A PRIZE FOR PEACE

Each year for over 100 years, one or two individuals or an organization is awarded the Nobel Peace Prize. The prize is given to someone who has done the best work for peace between nations. Previous winners have included South African president Nelson Mandela, activist Martin Luther King Jr., and U.S. president Theodore Roosevelt. Malala was nominated for this prize in 2013 and 2014.

Malala won the 2014 Nobel Peace Prize, sharing the prize with Indian activist Kailash Satyarthi. In addition to being the youngest person to win this prize, she became the first Pakistani to win it.

On December 10, 2014, she gave her Nobel Lecture to an audience in Oslo, Norway. She said, "Though I appear as one girl, one person…I am not a lone voice. I am many."

WOMEN WINNING THE NOBEL PRIZE

Malala was one of the many great women to win the Nobel Peace Prize. In 1979, Blessed Mother Teresa won the Nobel Prize for her work with the poor and sick in India. She founded the Missionaries of Charity and helped build homes for orphans and hospitals for the sick. In 1991, Aung San Suu Kyi won the Nobel Prize for her nonviolent fight for human rights and democracy in what's now Myanmar, but was once known as Burma.

Shown here is Malala holding her Nobel Peace Prize. By winning this prize, Malala showed that being young doesn't mean you can't change the world.

RAISING HER VOICE

Even as she became famous, Malala stayed true to her goals—she returned to school. Malala began attending the Edgbaston High School for Girls in Birmingham, England, in 2013. She strives to be a normal teenage schoolgirl. However, Malala has become someone normal girls and boys everywhere can look to for inspiration.

Malala is a role model for young people around the world. Her success and her story show that young people can make a difference. Even though the Taliban tried to silence her, Malala knew she had a choice: She could give in, or she could speak up. Malala continues to be heard across the globe as she continues her fight for education for every child.

IN HER WORDS

"Dear sisters and brothers, dear fellow children, we must work…not wait. Not just the politicians and the world leaders, we all need to contribute. …It is our duty."
Nobel Lecture delivered in Oslo, Norway, on December 10, 2014

In 2015, Malala opened a school for girls from Syria who had to escape to Lebanon because of armed conflicts in their home country.

TIMELINE

July 12, 1997: Malala is born.

September 2008: Malala gives her first speech.

January 3, 2009: Malala's first BBC blog is posted.

February 2009: Malala makes her first television appearance.

December 2011: Malala is awarded Pakistan's National Youth Peace Prize.

October 9, 2012: Malala is shot by a member of the Taliban.

July 12, 2013: Malala makes her first public appearance since she was attacked.

October 8, 2013: *I Am Malala* is published.

December 2013: Malala is awarded the United Nations Human Rights Prize.

October 21, 2014: Malala becomes the youngest person to accept the Liberty Medal.

December 10, 2014: Malala accepts the Nobel Peace Prize.

GLOSSARY

activism: Acting strongly in support of or against an issue.

blog: A website on which someone writes about personal opinions, activities, and experiences.

broadcast: Sent out using a televison, radio, or computer.

conservative: Believing in established and traditional practices in politics and society, and opposing change.

diplomat: A person who is skilled at talks between nations.

documentary: A nonfiction movie or television program presenting facts about an issue.

extremist: Someone who believes in or supports ideas that are very far from what most people consider correct or reasonable.

lecture: A speech given to a group of people about a particular subject.

memoir: A written account of one's life and the people and events of the times.

militant: Using force to support a cause or beliefs.

Pashtun: Belonging to a group of people from eastern and southern Afghanistan and parts of Pakistan.

terrorist: Having to do with using violence and fear to challenge an authority.

INDEX

WEBSITES

Due to the changing nature of Internet links, PowerKids Press has developed an
online list of websites related to the subject of this book. This site is updated regularly.
Please use this link to access the list: www.powerkidslinks.com/sprwmn/mal